TABLE OF CONTENTS

About The Author.................................1

Meet The Characters...................2

Chapter 1: Goal Setting.................6

Chapter 2: Words Have Power......10

Chapter 3: Self Love....................14

Chapter 4: My Strengths.............18

Chapter 5: I'm Working On It.......22

Chapter 6: Worry.........................26

Chapter 7: I am a Leader...........30

D.I.Y. Activities..........................34

Calm Down Strategies 35

Words of Affirmation................36

THIS BOOK IS DEDICATED TO:

♡ My mother and sister for your never ending support and encouragement.

♡ Ms. Tammy Wicks for making all of this possible.

♡ All the young children across the world reading this book.

ABOUT THE AUTHOR

Nykia Tucker IS A FIRST GRADE TEACHER IN PRINCE GEORGES COUNTY, MARYLAND WITH A DUAL-CERTIFICATION IN EARLY CHILDHOOD EDUCATION & SPECIAL EDUCATION. WHILE EARNING HER MASTERS IN EDUCATIONAL LEADERSHIP SHE BEGAN A BEHAVIOR PROGRAM IN ORDER TO IMPROVE THE SOCIAL AND EMOTIONAL HEALTH OF YOUNG CHILDREN IN HER COMMUNITY. SHE WAS INSPIRED TO TURN HER INSTRUCTIONAL LESSONS INTO A SELF-IMPROVEMENT BOOK WITH THE HOPES OF REACHING MANY CHILDREN IN COMMUNITIES ACROSS THE WORLD.

MEET THE

Hey! My name is Noah and I live in San Diego, California with my aunt, uncle and pet snake, Liam. I have autism and a super cool rock collection.

Konichiwa, I'm Kai! I was born in Tokyo, Japan. It's just me and my dad! Growing up I was bullied because of my freckles but I love them now.

Waa Gwaan! My name is Robyn and I live in Ochos Rios, Jamaica. I was adopted by my foster parents when I was a baby. I am on the honor roll in school and I love everything fashion!

G'day mate! My name is Isla and I live in Sydney, Australia with my grandparents. I love to hang out at the library and read cool books, especially now since I got my new glasses to help me see better.

CHARACTERS

Hola amigos! My name is Mateo and I am from Barcelona, Spain. I live with my mom and dog, Bleu. I have to wear a hearing aid because I was born partly deaf. I love to draw and ride my bike through the city.

Kedu! I'm Chidi from Lagos, Nigeria. I live with my 2 brothers, sister, mom and dad. I love to play football and listen to music. These hobbies help with my anxiety.

Namaste, I'm Prisha from Mumbai, India. I live with my parents, 2 siblings, grandparents, my aunt and 3 cousins. Last year, I was diagnosed with diabetes and now I take insulin.

LOOK WHERE

NORTH
AMERICA

SOUTH
AMERICA

AFRICA

WE ARE FROM PASSPORT

EUROPE

ASIA

AUSTRALIA

CHAPTER 1:
GOAL SETTING

2 CHRONICLES 15:7

Be strong and don't give up,
because you will get a reward
for your good work!

WHAT IS A GOAL?

A goal is something you want to achieve.

Here are some questions to think about to help you achieve a goal:

1. WHAT?

What is something you want to learn or improve on? What is it you would you do if you knew you could not fail?

2. WHY?

Why did you choose this goal? Is this goal going to help you be a better version of yourself? Can this goal help other people too?

3. HOW?

How are you going to reach your goal? What are the important steps you need to complete to achieve your goal?

4. REVIEW & REFLECT

How is it going? Is there anything you need to change?

Now it's your turn! When you write your goals down, you are more likely to achieve it..

MY GOALS

My goal is:

The purpose of my goal is:

Three things I can do to achieve this goal:

1.

2.

3.

Check here when you meet your goal

what if these leaders gave up on their goals ?

OPRAH WINFREY

Don't **QUIT**

HELEN KELLER

→ Remember your "WHY"!

→ Every time you complete a step you are that much closer to achieving your goal.

→ It may take a few tries to get it right. That is OK!

→ Tell yourself, "I can do it!"

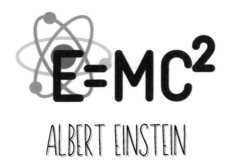

MICHAEL JORDAN

$E=MC^2$

ALBERT EINSTEIN

BARACK OBAMA

CHAPTER 2:
WORDS HAVE POWER

EPHESIANS 4:32
Be Kind and loving. Forgive each other the same as God forgives you.

WORDS HAVE POWER?

YES, WORDS HAVE SO MUCH POWER!

what if...

You're at the playground and kids say hello and smile at you?

You're at the playground and kids ignore you. Some say mean things.

which one would make you feel appreciated?
which one would make you feel unappreciated?

→ Think about your words before you say them.

→ Saying unkind words can hurt someone's feelings.

→ Saying kind words can make someone feel happy.

Write or draw about a time when someone used
Kind words and made you feel appreciated?

_____

_____

_____

_____

_____

Write or draw about a time when someone used
unKind words that made you feel unappreciated?

_____

_____

_____

_____

THINK BEFORE YOU SPEAK

→ The words you say are important, so be sure to <u>think</u> about your words before you <u>speak</u> them out loud.

→ **Ask yourself this:** "Is what I am about to say Kind and helpful, or will it hurt their feelings? How would I feel if someone said this to me?

→ Think of a time you have said hurtful words to someone? How do you think this made them feel? ☹

→ Think of a time you have said Kind words to someone? How do you think this made them feel? ☺

CHAPTER 3:

SELF - LOVE

PSALM 139: 13-14

You formed the way I think and feel. You put me together in my mother's womb. I praise you because you made me in such a wonderful way.

SELF-LOVE

what does it mean to love yourself?

It means that I am my own best friend. I love myself even when I make mistakes.

I can show self-love through <u>affirmations</u>:

I am amazing.

I am smart.

I am important.

I am valuable.

I am kind.

I am confident.

I am loved.

what do you love about yourself?
write all the things you love about
yourself in the heart.

REMEMBER!

You are wonderfully made. There is no one else like you!

Whenever you are feeling sad, look in the mirror and remind yourself how much of a great person you are!

CHAPTER 4:
MY STRENGTHS

PHILIPPIANS 4:13

Christ is the one who gives
me the strength I need to do
whatever I must do.

WHAT ARE STRENGTHS?

A strength is something that you are good at doing!

What are your strengths at school?
(Maybe you are hardworking and patient.)

What are your strengths at home?
(Maybe you are organized and responsible.)

What are your strengths with your friendships?
(Maybe you are gentle and caring.)

(Your Name Here)

It is important to understand your own strengths. List one strength for each letter of your name or draw a picture of yourself and write your strengths around it.

YOUR STRENGTHS

A positive mindset can help you improve on your strengths

When you think this:

I am afraid to try new things.

I quit, this is too hard.

What if I make a mistake?

My friends are smarter than me.

I do not look like my friends.

I am not good enough.

I do not like school.

You can say:

When I make a mistake, I will learn and get better.

I will never give up, I got this!

If I make a mistake, I can try again.

I will work hard and study.

I am perfect just the way I am.

I tried my best and will keep practicing.

I will have fun at school and enjoy learning.

POSITIVE THOUGHTS create a POSITIVE YOU

CHAPTER 5:

I'M WORKING ON IT

PROVERBS 3 : 5 - 6
Trust the Lord, and don't
depend on your own knowledge.
With every step you take, think
about what he wants, and he
will help you go the right way.

WHAT ARE YOUR CHALLENGES?

Challenges are areas that you need to work on. There is always room for improvement.

It is important to Know your challenges just as much as you Know your strengths.

Knowing your challenges help you understand yourself a little better.

Think of some things you need to work on at school? Are there some things you need to work on at home... or with your friends?

What is one skill you need to work on:

_____

_____

_____

_____

What are 3 things you can do to get better:

1 _____

_____

2 _____

_____

3 _____

_____

I'M WORKING ON IT

Understanding your challenges are the missing pieces to the puzzle. It helps you to grow as a person. Once you find your skills you need to improve, slowly work towards getting better. Remember to use your strengths too and focus on the positive. There is so much you can do when you know yourself.

CHAPTER 6:

WORRY

DEUTERONOMY 31:8

The Lord will lead you. He is
with you and will not fail you
or leave you. Don't worry.
Don't be afraid!

HOW BIG IS YOUR WORRY?

Not all worries are the same size!

Does your worry feel small, medium, or big?

A small worry could be feeling nervous before a big test, getting a shot at the doctor, or trying out for a sports team.

A big worry could be that your family is moving to a new state and now you will have a new home and a new school.

MY WORRIES

Let's think of some small, medium and big worries.

small

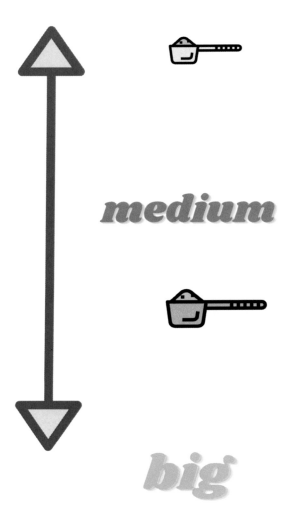
medium

big

DON'T WORRY

It is important to realize the size of your worry. This will allow adults in your life to better understand how to help you and make you feel better.

Don't cry over spilled milk!

CHAPTER 7:
I AM A LEADER

1 TIMOTHY 4:12

You are young, but don't let anyone treat you as if you are not important. Be an example to show others how they should live. Show them by what you say, by the way you live, and by your love.

what does it mean to be a leader?
LEADERSHIP

A leader is someone who helps you. They inspire and motivate you to do better.

Who is a leader in your life?
(Your parents, teacher, or coach)

What makes them a leader?
(They encourage you and teach you new things)

How can you be a leader?

Draw and write about how you can be a leader at home, school, or in your community.

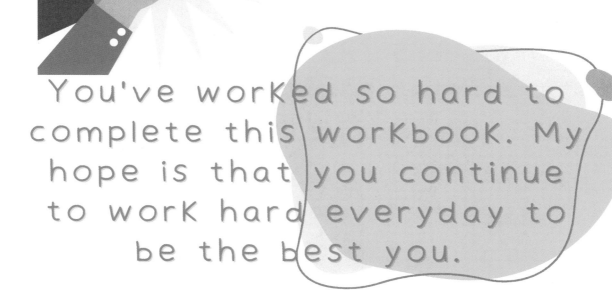

You've worked so hard to complete this workbook. My hope is that you continue to work hard everyday to be the best you.

what is the biggest lesson you have learned?

DIY ACTIVITIES

HOW TO MAKE A STRESS BALL

1. Stretch out balloon
2. Place a funnel into balloon
3. Slowly fill balloon with rice or flour
4. Remove funnel and let out air
5. Tie balloon into a Knot & Squeeze

- balloon
- funnel
- rice or flour

- -

HOW TO MAKE A CALM DOWN JAR

1. Fill a jar with water
2. Add 1-2 drops of food coloring
3. Add glitter and mini pom poms
4. Glue top to jar to avoid leaks
5. Shake & Enjoy

- jar
- glue
- water
- food coloring
- glitter
- mini pom poms

CALM DOWN STRATEGIES

Count to 10

Take deep breaths

Stretch out my arms and legs

Talk to a friend

write about how you feel

Draw about how you feel

Listen to music

Take a walk

Squeeze a ball

Say something kind about yourself

WORDS OF AFFIRMATION

USE THESE WORDS TO REMIND YOURSELF HOW REMARKABLE YOU ARE!

I AM...

somebody	unique
smart	valued
beautiful / handsome	appreciated
kind	loved
funny	special
strong	helpful
hard working	proud of myself

Your Tomorrow Starts Today

LET YOUR LIGHT SHINE !